Life Choices

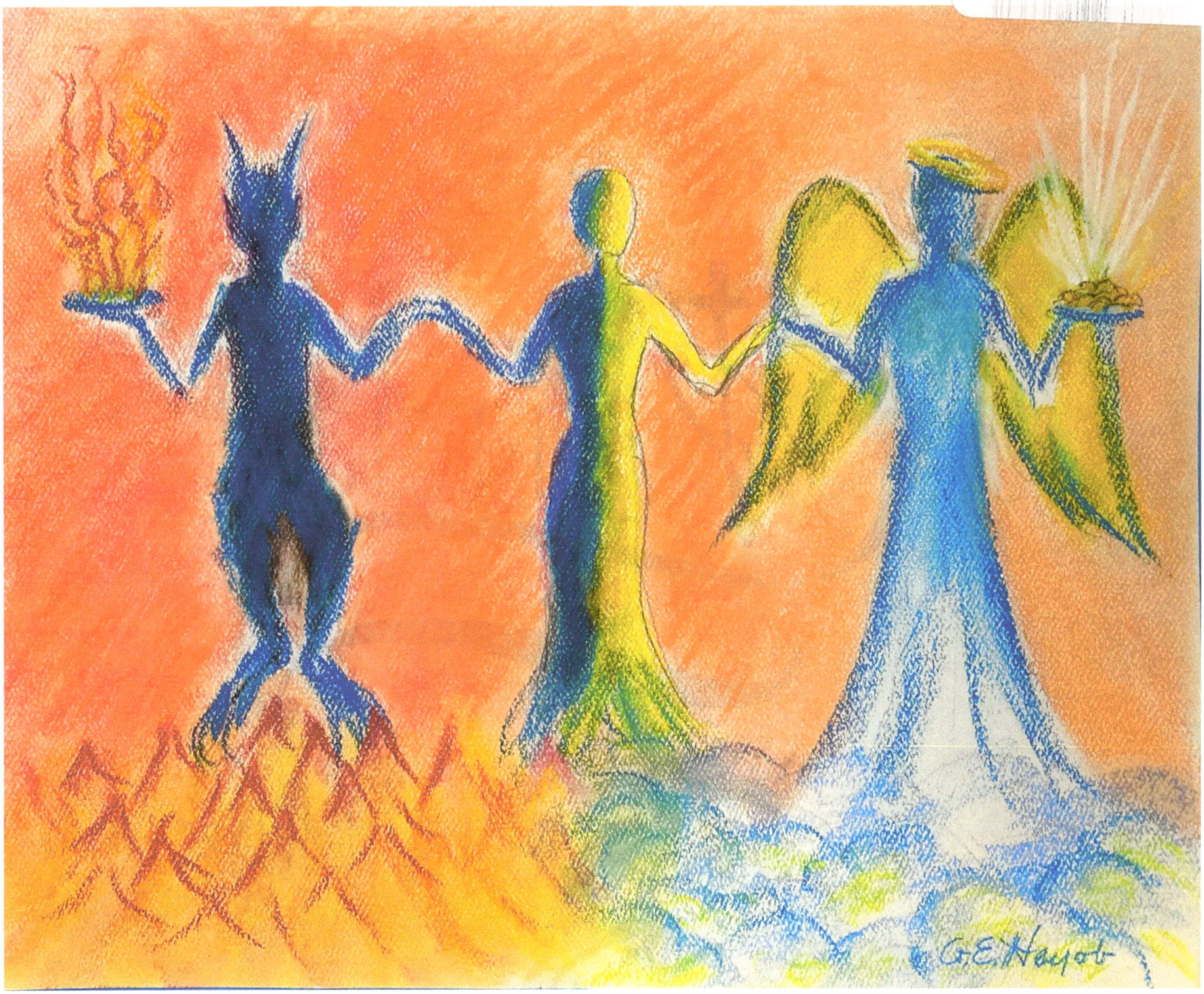

by GE Hayob

Sensitive Material: Parental Preview Recommended
for ages 13 and up

I've been given an incredible opportunity—Angel Studios has invited me to submit a pilot or trailer for potential film production. While nothing is guaranteed yet (which is why contributions aren't refundable), this could be the first step toward bringing my story to life in a powerful way.

But I can't do it alone—I need your help to make it happen.

This project isn't about glorifying me. It's about shining a light on what God has done in my life and inspiring young girls to make choices rooted in faith and purpose.

Together, we can create something meaningful—a story of transformation from a disillusioned young girl to a confident, faith-filled woman.

We've set up several contribution tiers to help fund the production of the pilot. Each level comes with its own unique impact, and every gift helps move us one step closer to the screen.

Let's bring this story to life—together.

Life Choices

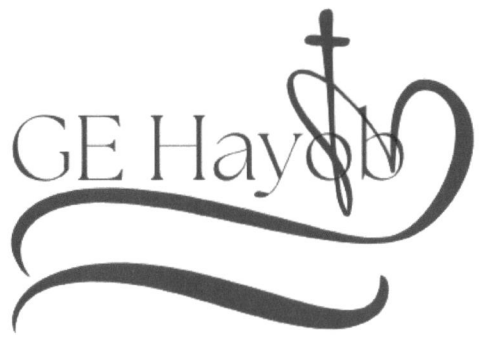

by GE Hayob

Sensitive Material: parental preview recommended
for ages 13 and up

Email: GEHayob@gmail.com
ETSY: LifeChoicesStudio
Website: https://gehayob.wordpress.com/

Revision - December 2025

Donations going to various Christian Organizations and Charities

Introduction

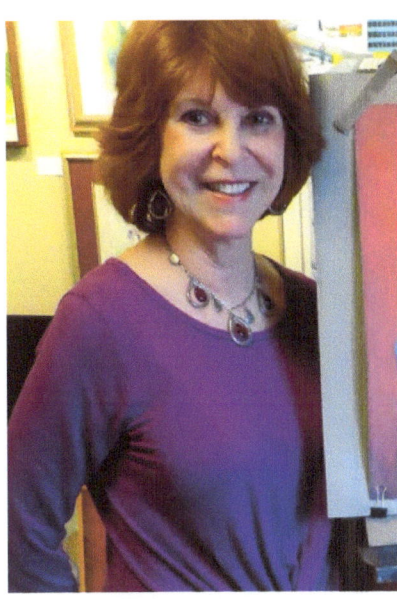

I have always loved art as a child but got serious about it after I became a flight attendant and visited famous museums, especially the Louvre in Paris.

My life as a flight attendant was glamorous, where I met presidents, the rich, and the famous. On my first trip out of the country, I took a trip around the world. With every luxury I could imagine, I felt empty and, least of all, happy. During this time, I made my share of wrong choices. I talked to a fellow flight attendant who directed me to a pastor who helped me understand the true meaning of life. I found God at home alone in my apartment reading the New Testament. I started in the gospel of John and the red words of Jesus jumped off of the page. After surrendering my life to Christ, this new understanding of life gave me a purpose I never had before. I realized that God is not looking for religion, but a relationship.

I started doing art with a passion. I loved capturing the human face, so I began doing portraits. I was commissioned for my first portrait in 1979. I also did a wide variety of other subjects in various mediums. I was commissioned to do over 3,000 pieces and have work in 9 museums. I have taught art in many venues and on cruise ships around the world. My art career was orchestrated by God since I never had classes in school nor do I have an art degree. About 10 years ago, I felt the Lord leading me to paint to glorify Him. So, I began doing what I felt He was leading me to do. The avant-garde pastels may appear radical and unconventional, but they are true nonetheless.

After retiring, my husband and I began traveling to Florida during the winter months. As we spent time with our new senior friends at restaurants, our servers were typically young people. Remembering my young adult years without clear direction and purpose, I felt moved to talk with them and see where they felt their lives were headed. Most have lost their moral compass. I wanted to help them make better choices. We led a small group through our church and counseled people there and also went into prisons to minister for several years.

I checked into being a faith-based life coach, but it was going to require a lot of time and effort, much more than I knew. Then I realized God gave me a gift to offer some thought-provoking images through my art. It was then that I felt the Lord was telling me to put these images into a book. This book is about the battle of the flesh and the spirit. It is my hope that someone will be helped to see the light through this art.

Can You See?

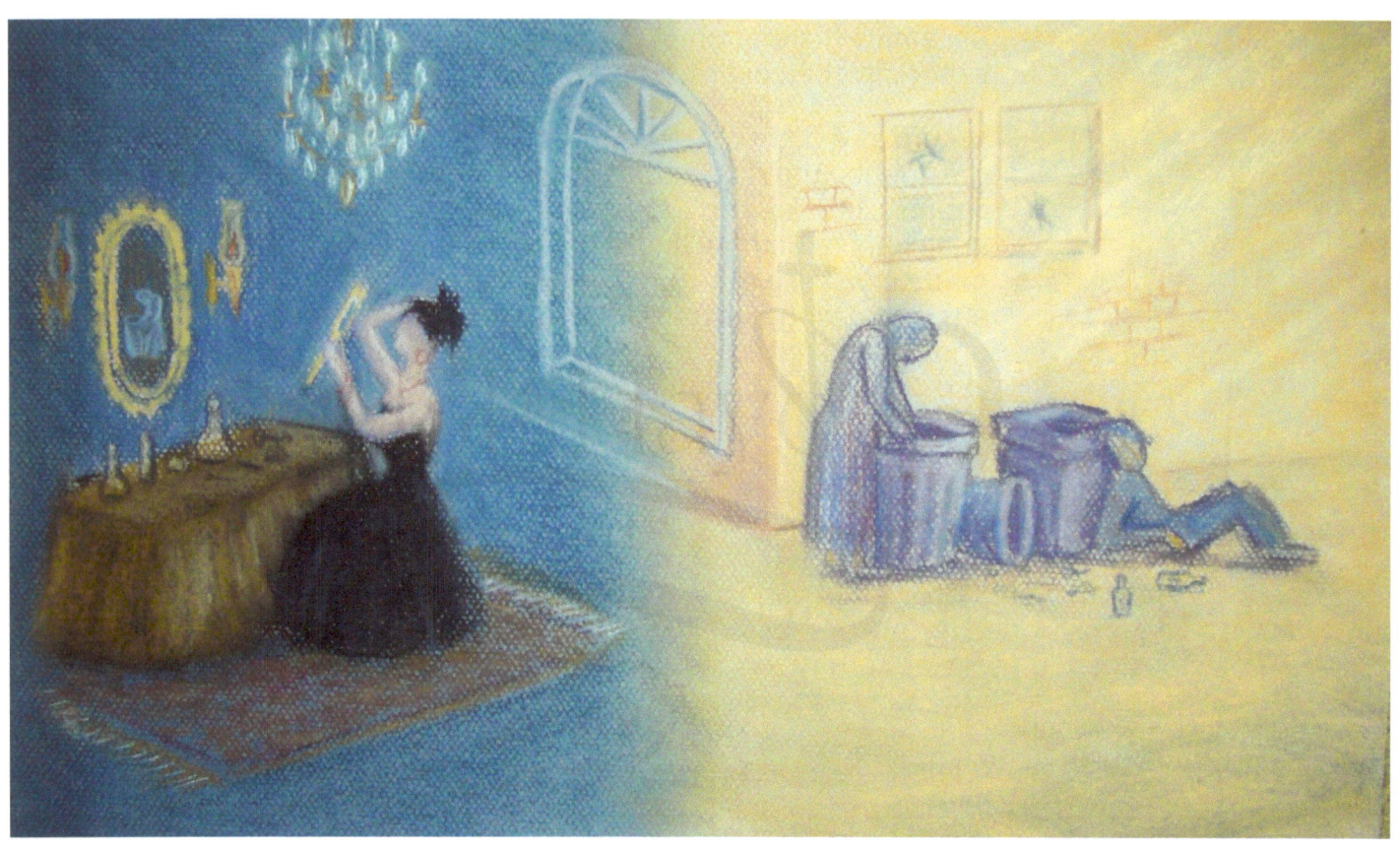

The rich lady is so engrossed with herself, she can't see the poor and needy outside of her window. Open your eyes to the needs of others around you. Your purpose on earth is more than just serving yourself.

Proverbs 31:20   1 John 3:17

Dollar Tree

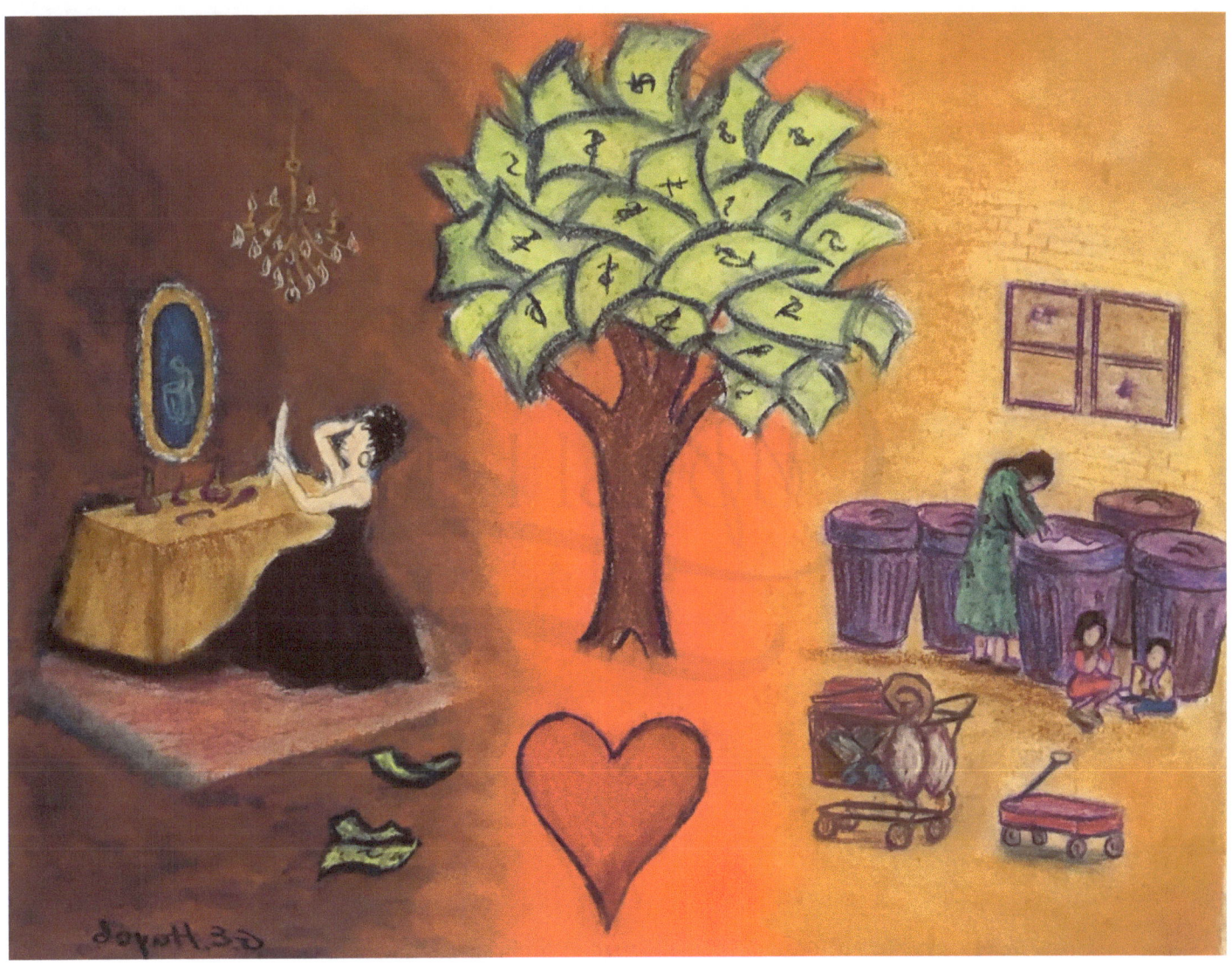

The love of money can cause us to be so focused on ourselves, we can not focus on anyone else, especially helping the less fortunate.

Proverbs 28:8   2 Timothy 3:1-2

Paper Dolls

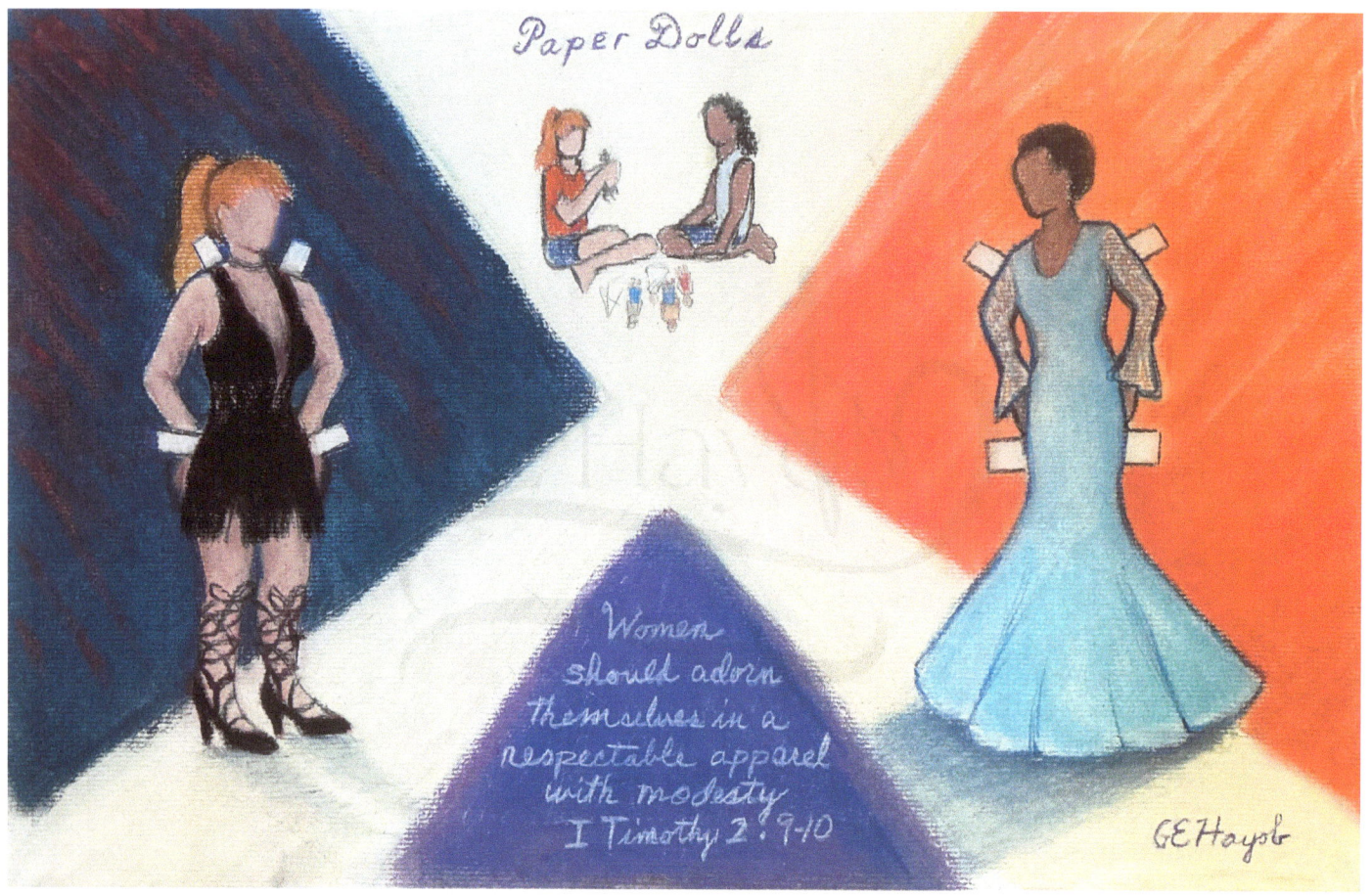

Ladies, you can dress immodestly and gain the wrong kind of attention,
or you can dress modestly and attract someone to your heart,
not just your body.

Proverbs 31:30   1 Corinthians 6:19-20

What Does it Cost?

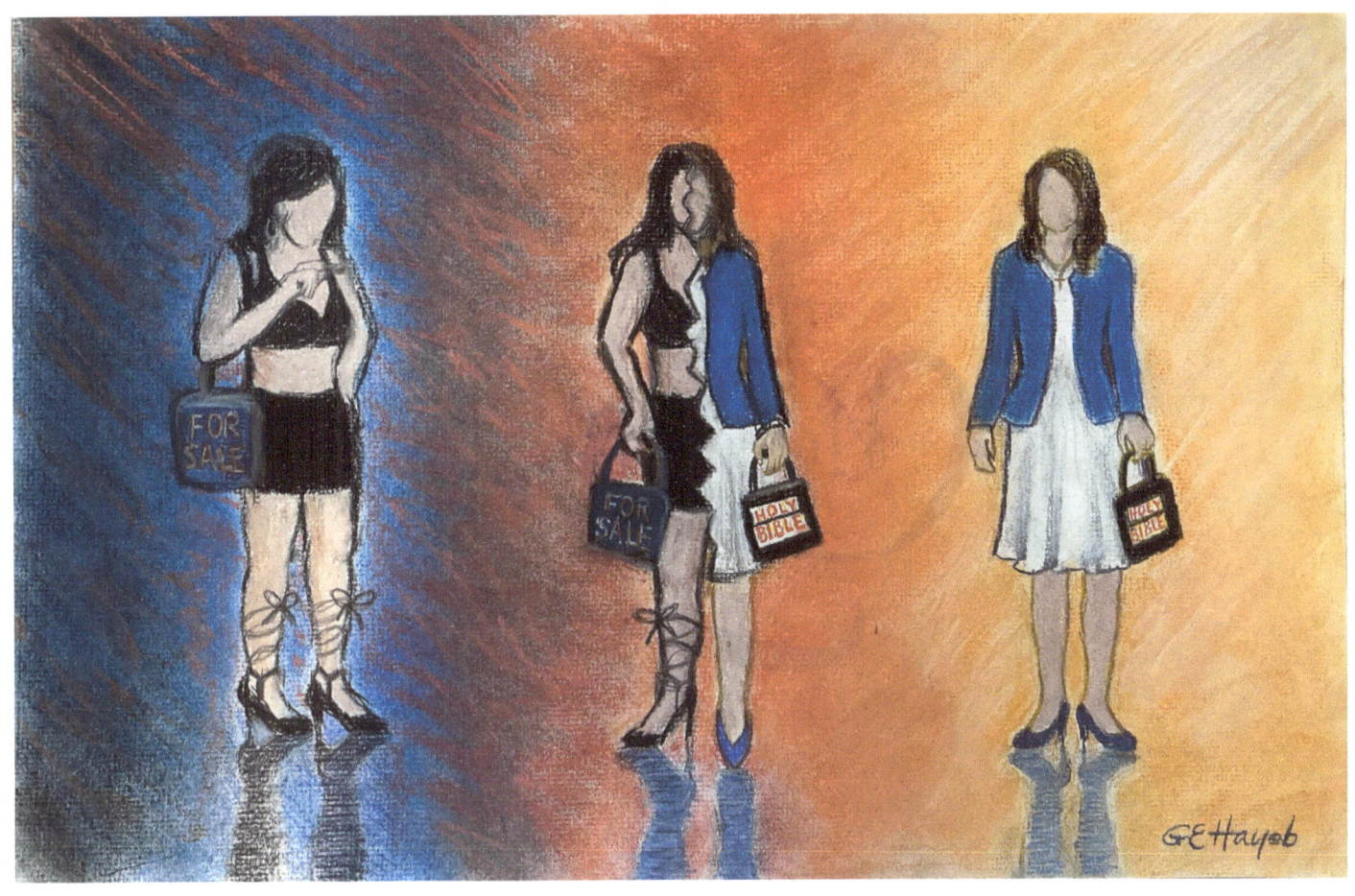

You were created in the image of God. You are adored by Him.
Do not sacrifice your soul to the world when it does not value you the way God does.

Proverbs 10:2   Luke 9:25

Which Way to Go?

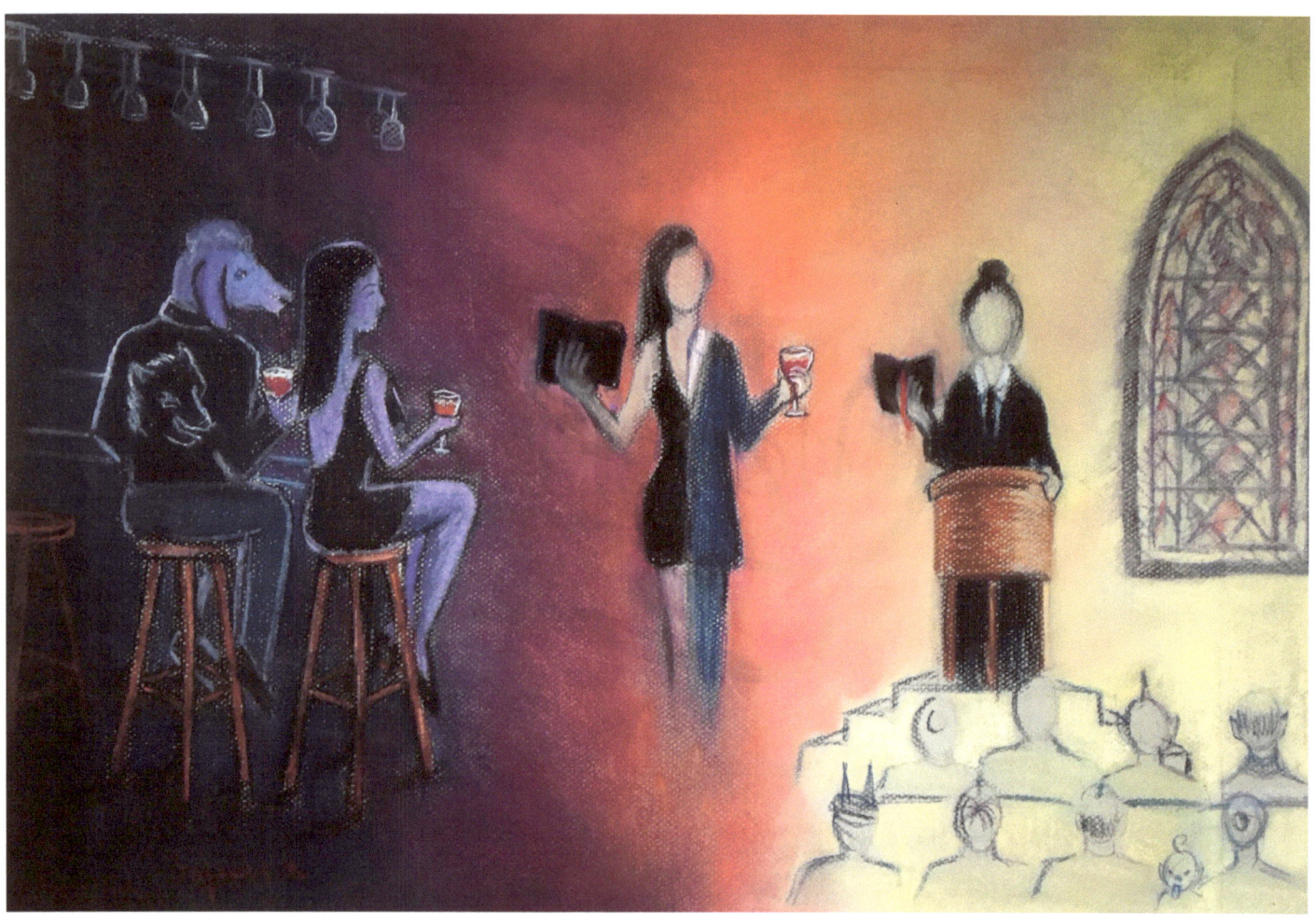

The world is deceiving. The lure of the dark side leads us to believe that we can have more fun if we have a few drinks with Mr. Wrong.

Colossians 2:8   1 John 2:16

Liquid Lies

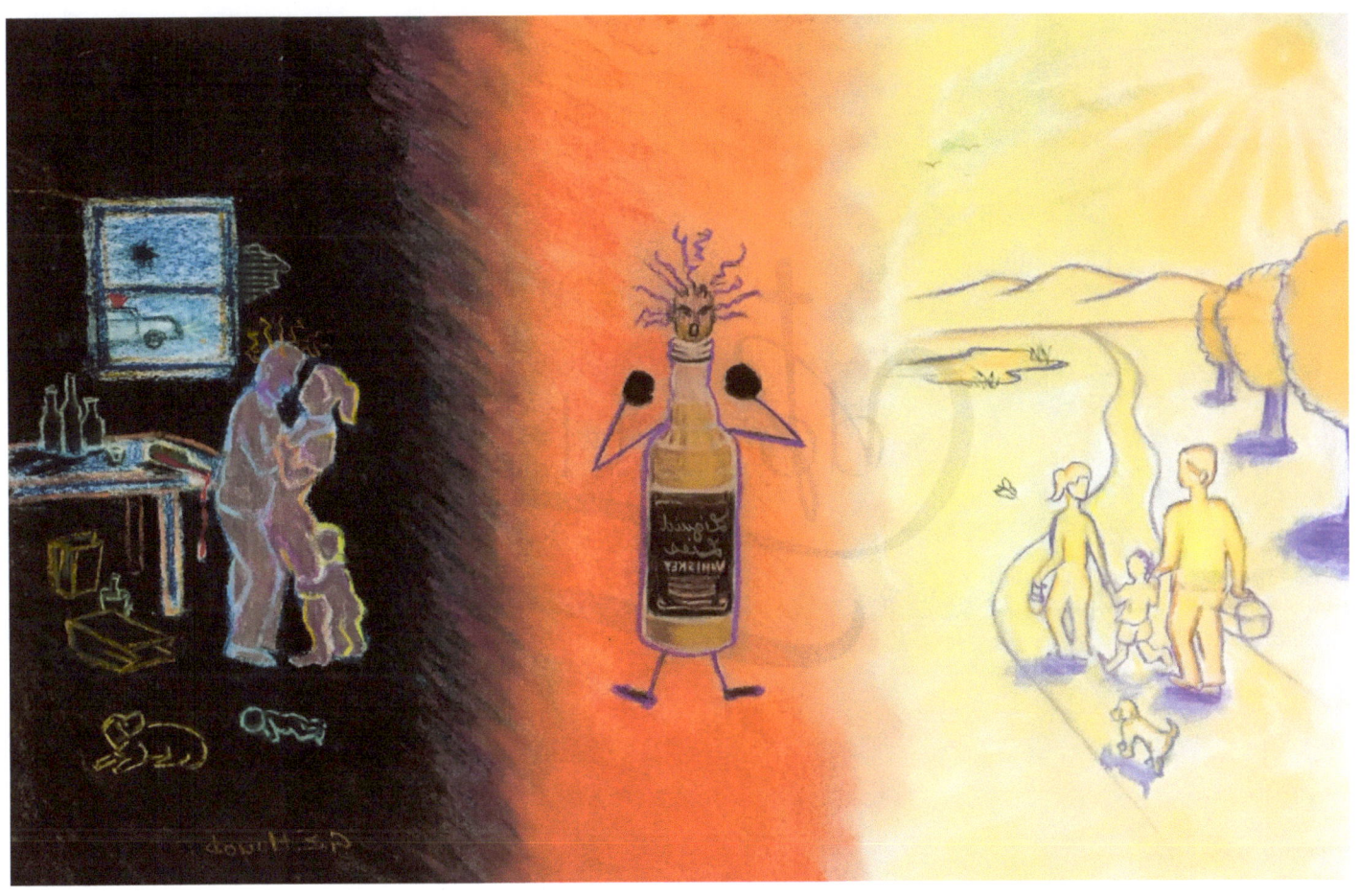

Joe Daniels is caught in the bottle. When he's sober, he is a nice guy, but when he is drunk he is evil. Alcoholic drink is called the wine of violence.

Proverbs 4:17   Ephesians 5:18

Monkey on My Back

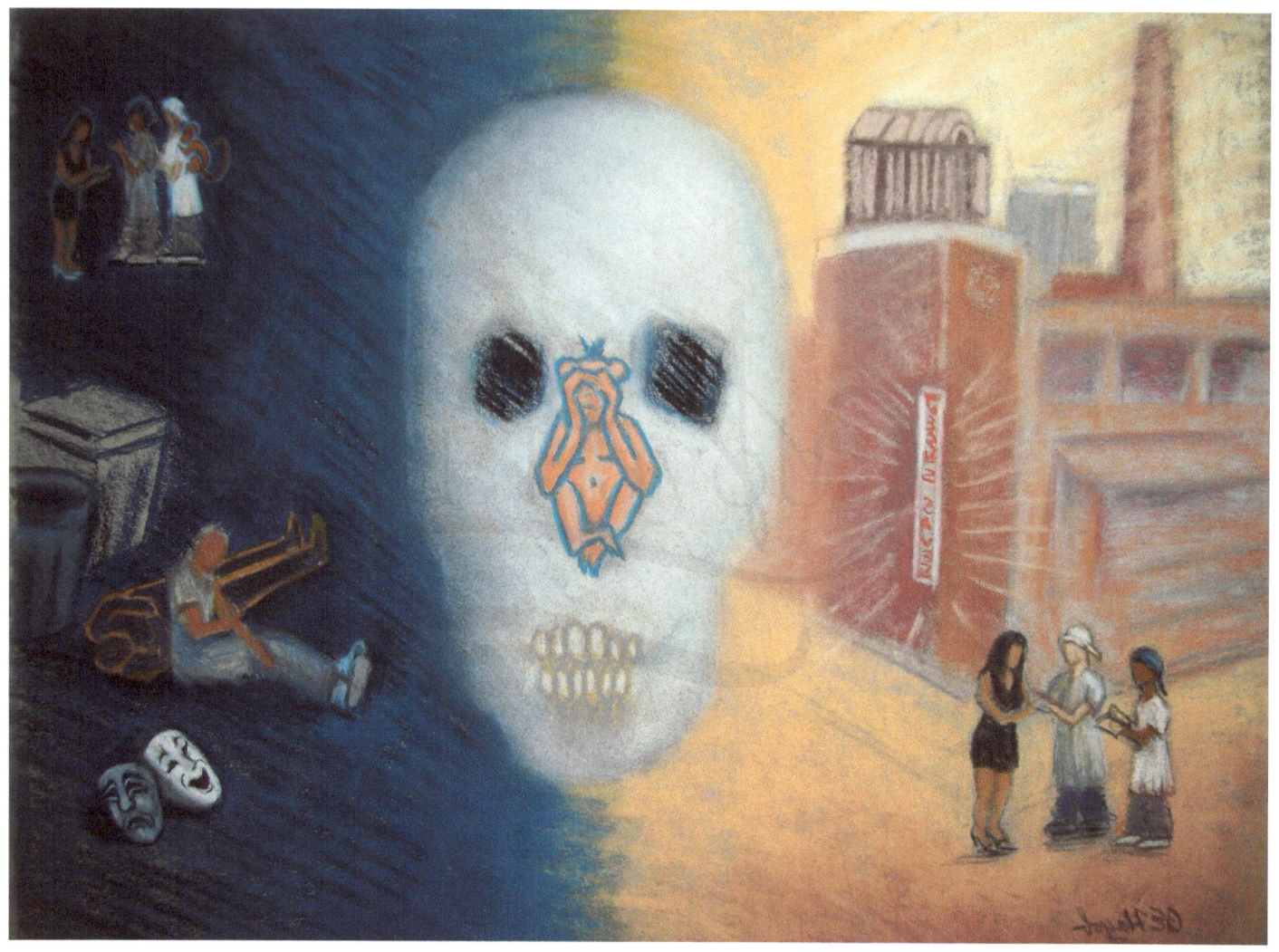

Drugs will make a monkey out of you. Addictions hide your pain instead of bringing it to the surface. You can be healed and set free to live a fulfilling life by sharing the love of Christ.

John 10:10   Ephesians 2:10

Julie's Story

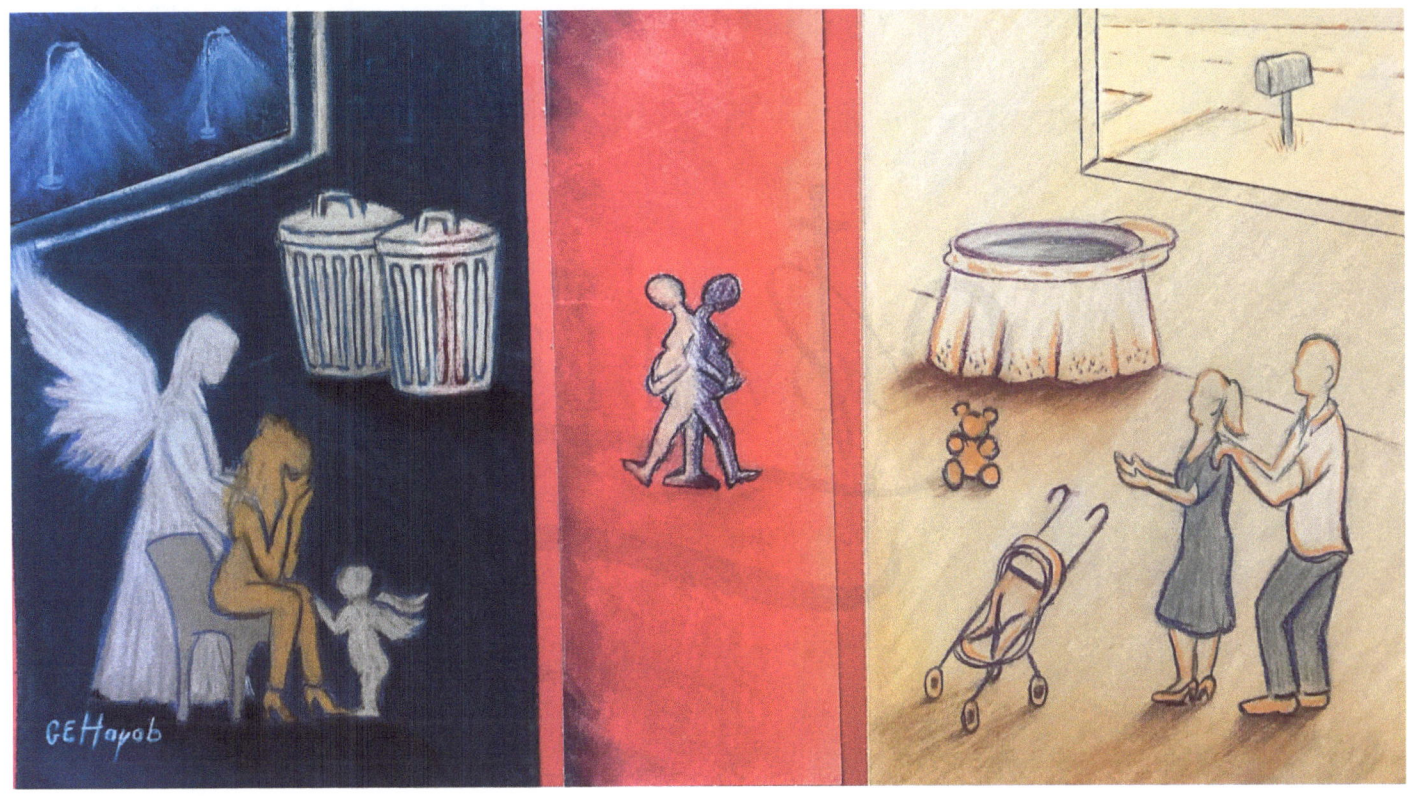

In 1979, at the age of sixteen, I found out I was pregnant. I was too afraid and ashamed to tell my parents, so I only confided in my boyfriend and friends. Everything in me wanted to keep my baby, but everyone I talked to about it would tell me differently, "You have no choice but to have an abortion."

A friend who once had an abortion helped me make an appointment and drove me to the abortion clinic when the day arrived. Looking back, if one person had said to me that it was my choice and I could keep the baby, I would have changed my mind instantly.

After arriving and checking in, a woman called me and several girls to a back room with pictures on the wall of what looked like groups of cells. Pointing at the pictures, she said, "This is what we will be removing today; a mass of cells, much like a tumor." Today, I now know that those pictures were of the outside of the embryonic sac and that the baby is developed to the point of having eyes, a nose, a beating heart, and measurable brain waves by 6 to 8 weeks.

Soon after, I was ushered, alone, into a cold, gray room. As I sat there waiting for the abortionist to come in, I heard a voice, "Run! Get out of here!" I stood up, looking around, and saw no one. I paced the room for 10 to 15 minutes, wanting to leave so badly. As I sat back down on the table, I heard the voice a second time, "Run, get out of here!" However, the fear of what my parents, peers, and boyfriend would think held me down on that table. During the excruciatingly painful procedure, which seemed to last forever, I heard the abortionist yell at his assistant, "How far along is she? This baby is fighting me!" In that instant, I knew I had been lied to and that my 12-week old preborn child had fought for his life.

Anger, which I'd never felt before with such intensity, invaded my life like a dark, oppressive cloud. I was angry at everyone, especially myself. For the next three years, I lived in a very destructive way. I didn't care if I lived or died. I just wanted to numb the pain I felt.

When I found out that I was pregnant for a second time at the age of 19, this child gave me a reason to live. I received the same advice from all of my friends, that I should get an abortion. I knew that I would never do such a horrible thing again.

The sorrow of his loss never goes away. Nevertheless, with God's mercy, help, and forgiveness, the intensity of the anger and hurt has eased over time. What gives me some comfort is knowing that my nine children that followed have been saved from the brutal death of abortion because of my first child's short but valiant fight for life. So, I follow his example and the example of my Lord and Savior Jesus Christ and fight any way I can for the lives of innocent babies and the souls of their confused mothers. The blood of Jesus has set me free from any guilt or stain.

Over 63.5 million babies have been aborted since 1973 to date.

Psalms 139:13-16   1 John 1:9

New Creation

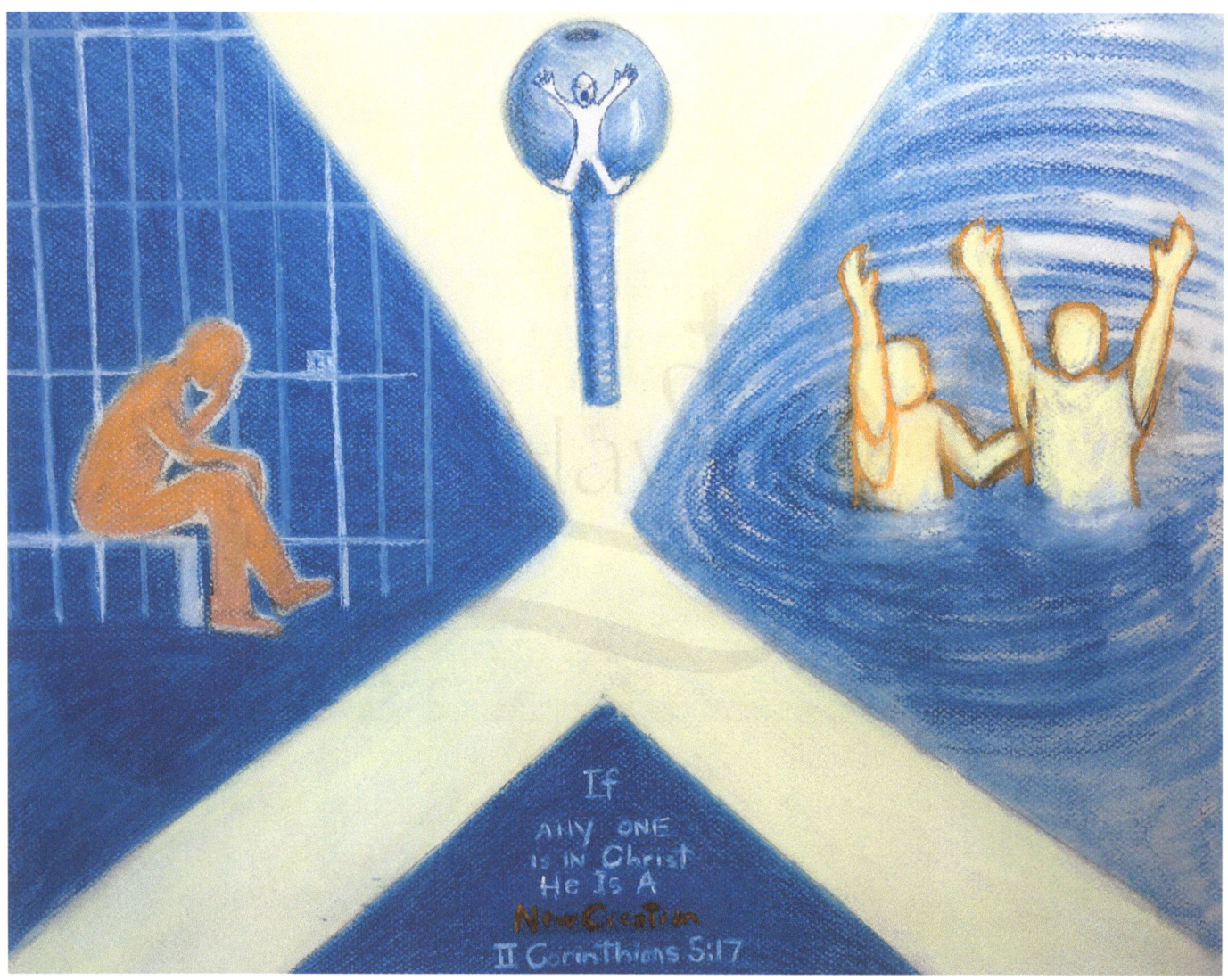

An addiction to alcohol or drugs is like being chained to an evil master. Only through Jesus Christ can we gain freedom and become a "New Creation".

Proverbs 29:6   1 Corinthians 7:21-23

Strong Drink is Raging

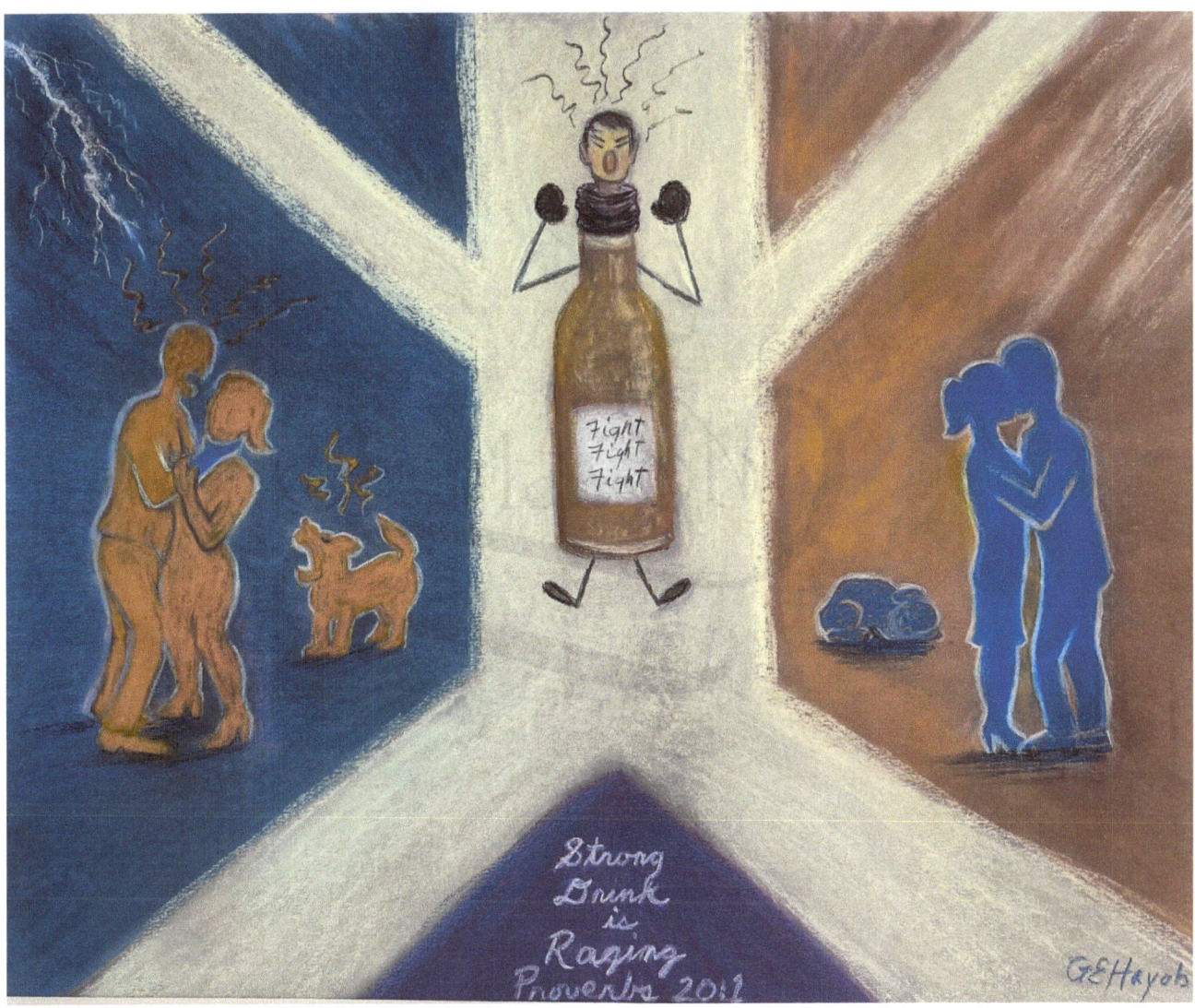

An abundance of alcohol can cloud your thinking and inhibit your judgment. When your mind isn't focused and clear you can feel physically and emotionally trapped.

Proverbs 20:1   Ephesians 5:18

Blind Sided

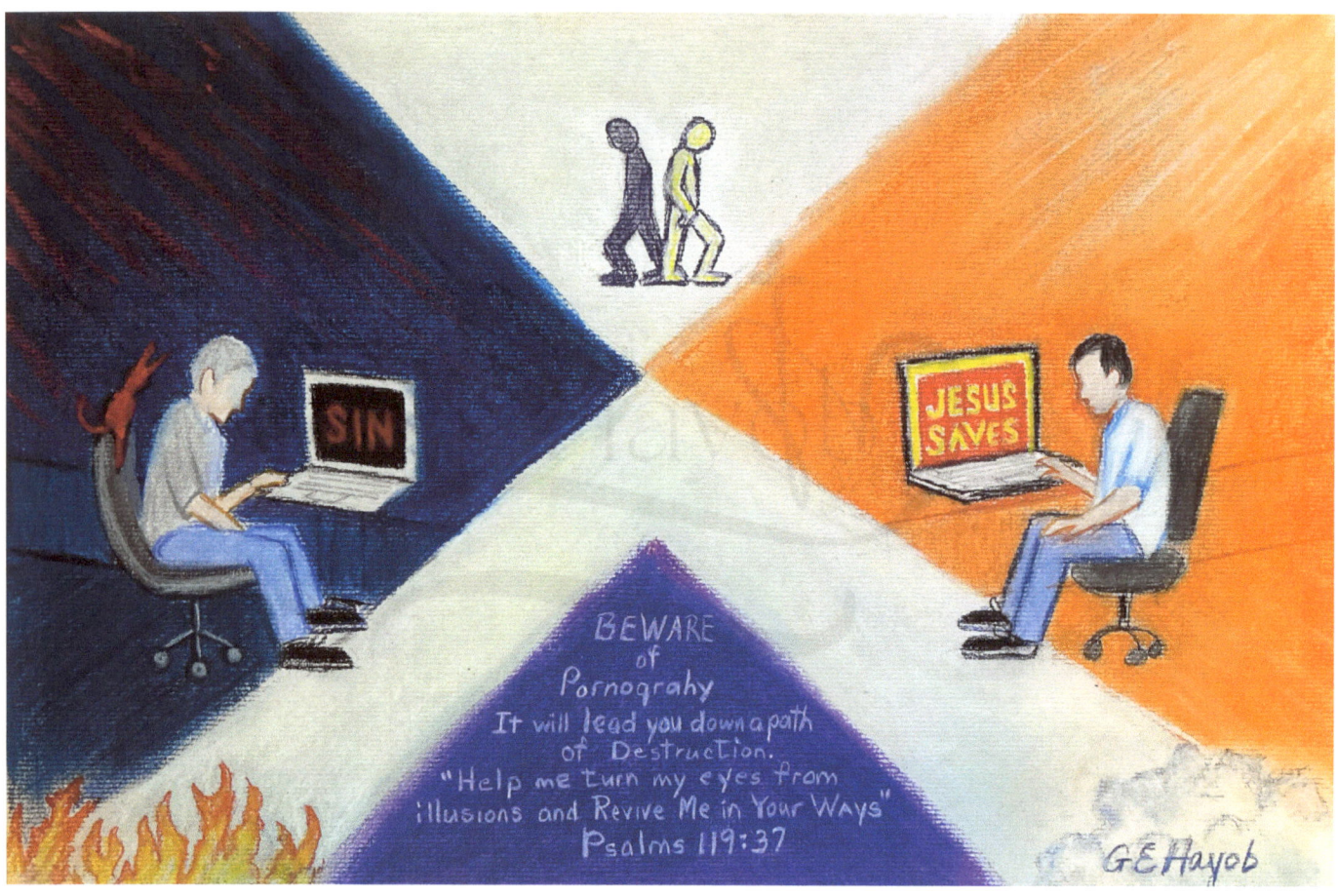

Pornography is an addiction that enslaves just as any other. Not only can it destroy your mind by filling it with lies, it can destroy your relationships.

Proverbs 5:8-9   Matthew 5:28

The Eyes of the Lord are Everywhere

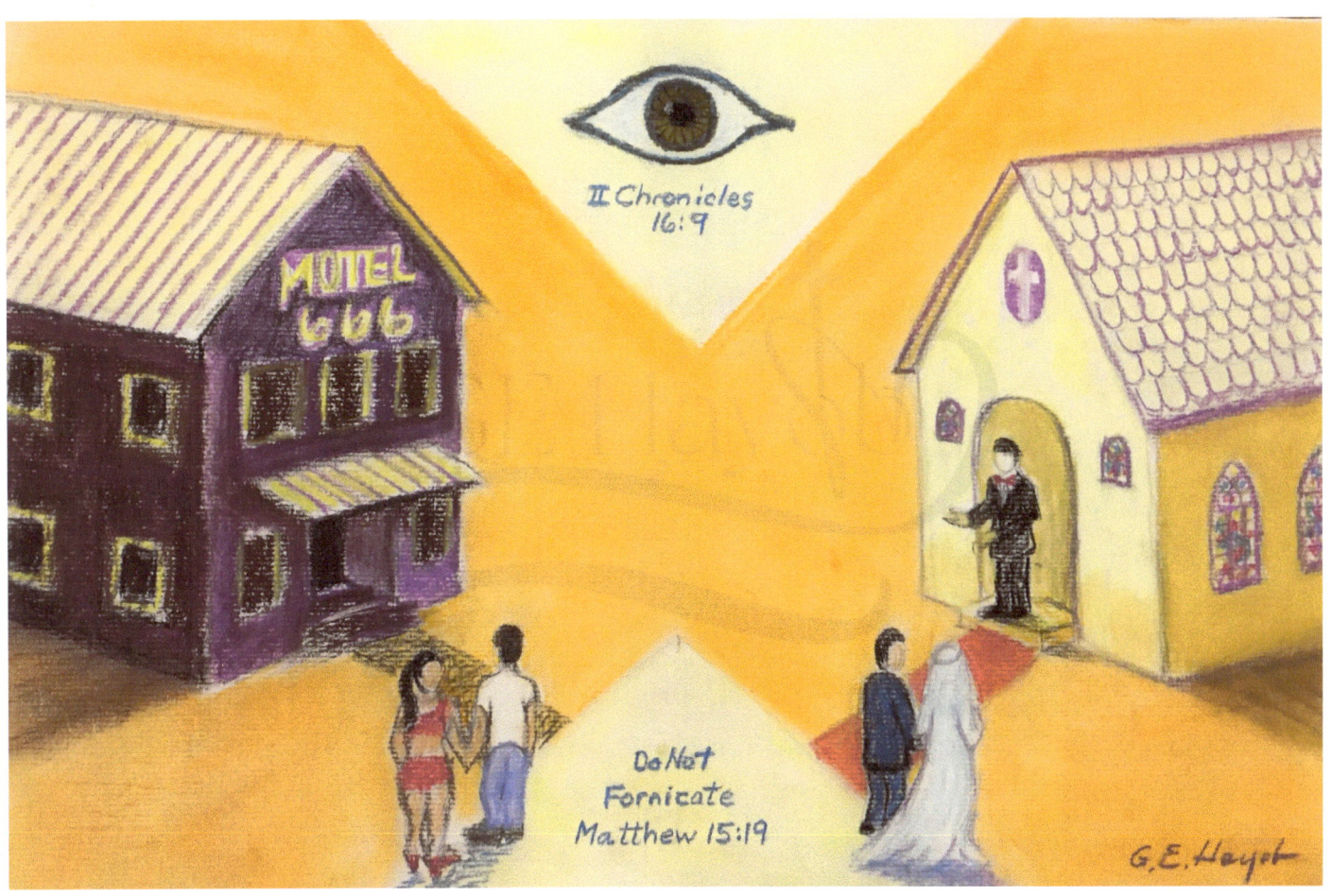

God wants your life to be pure before him, but also for your marriage partner. He can make your life holy and clean as He prepares you for your marriage vows.

Proverbs 22:11   Hebrews 13:4

Two-Faced

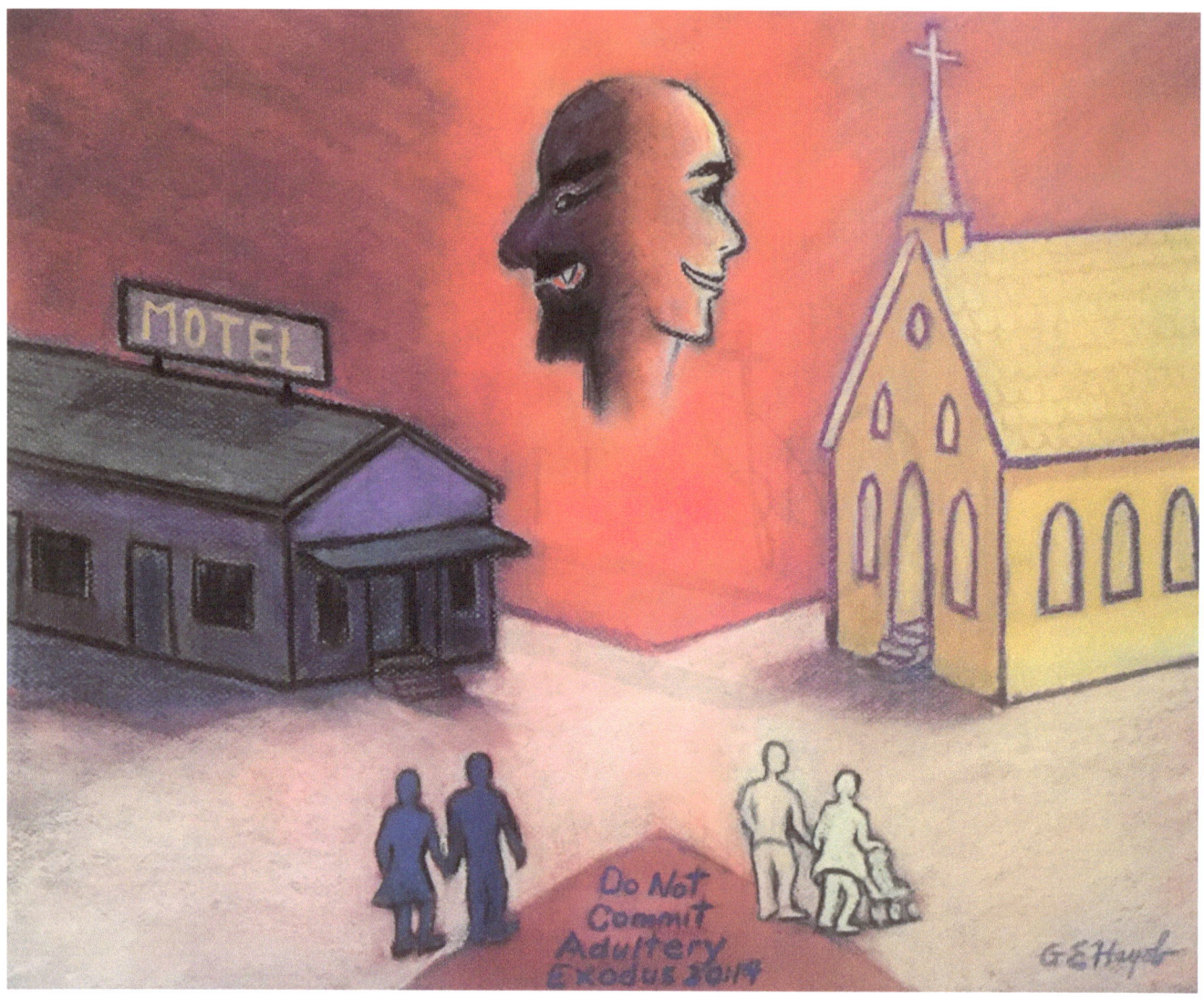

The enemy of our souls wants you to believe that adultery is okay by telling you the other woman will make you happy. The devil is a liar! Listen to the voice within you. God is trying to speak His truth to you.

Proverbs 6:32-33   Galatians 5:19-22

The Greatest of These is Love

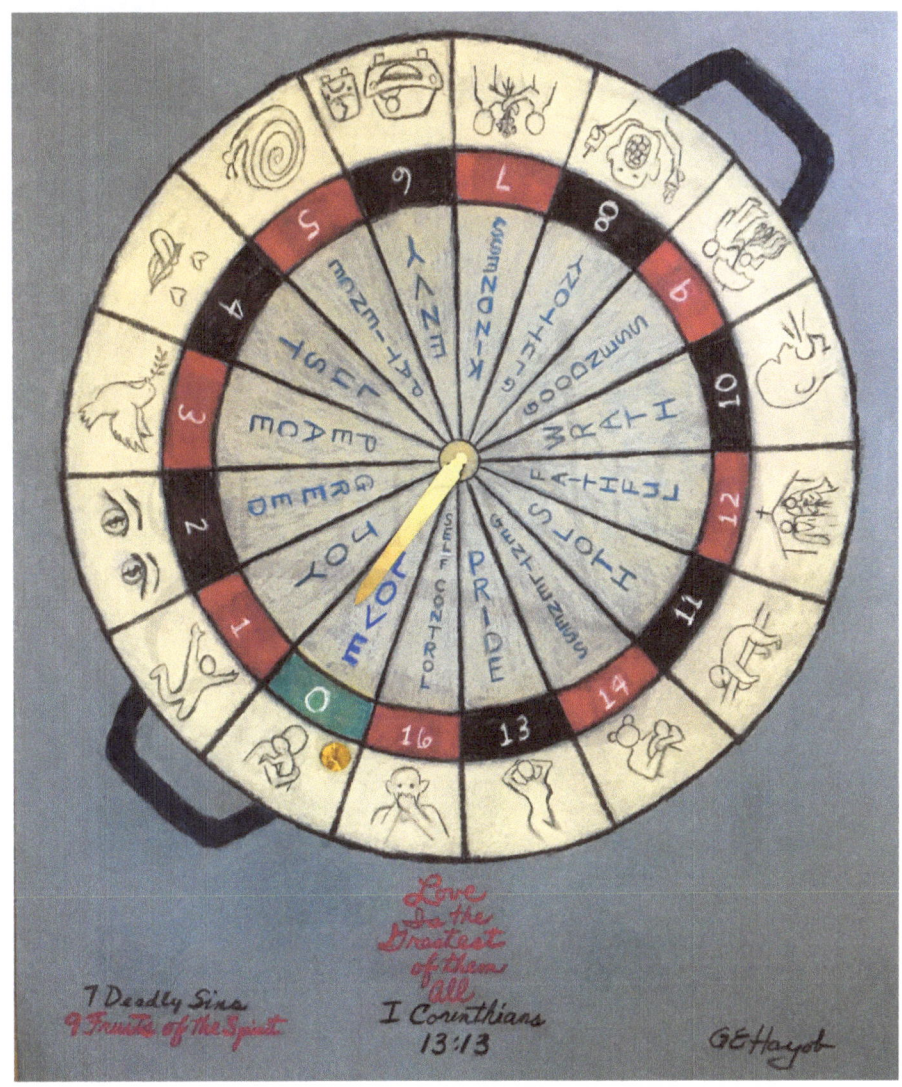

This image shows seven deadly sins and nine fruits of the spirit. Where will it land for you? I hope on love, because love is the greatest of them all.

Proverbs 20:27-28   1 Corinthians 13:4-13

Better Choice Pharmacy

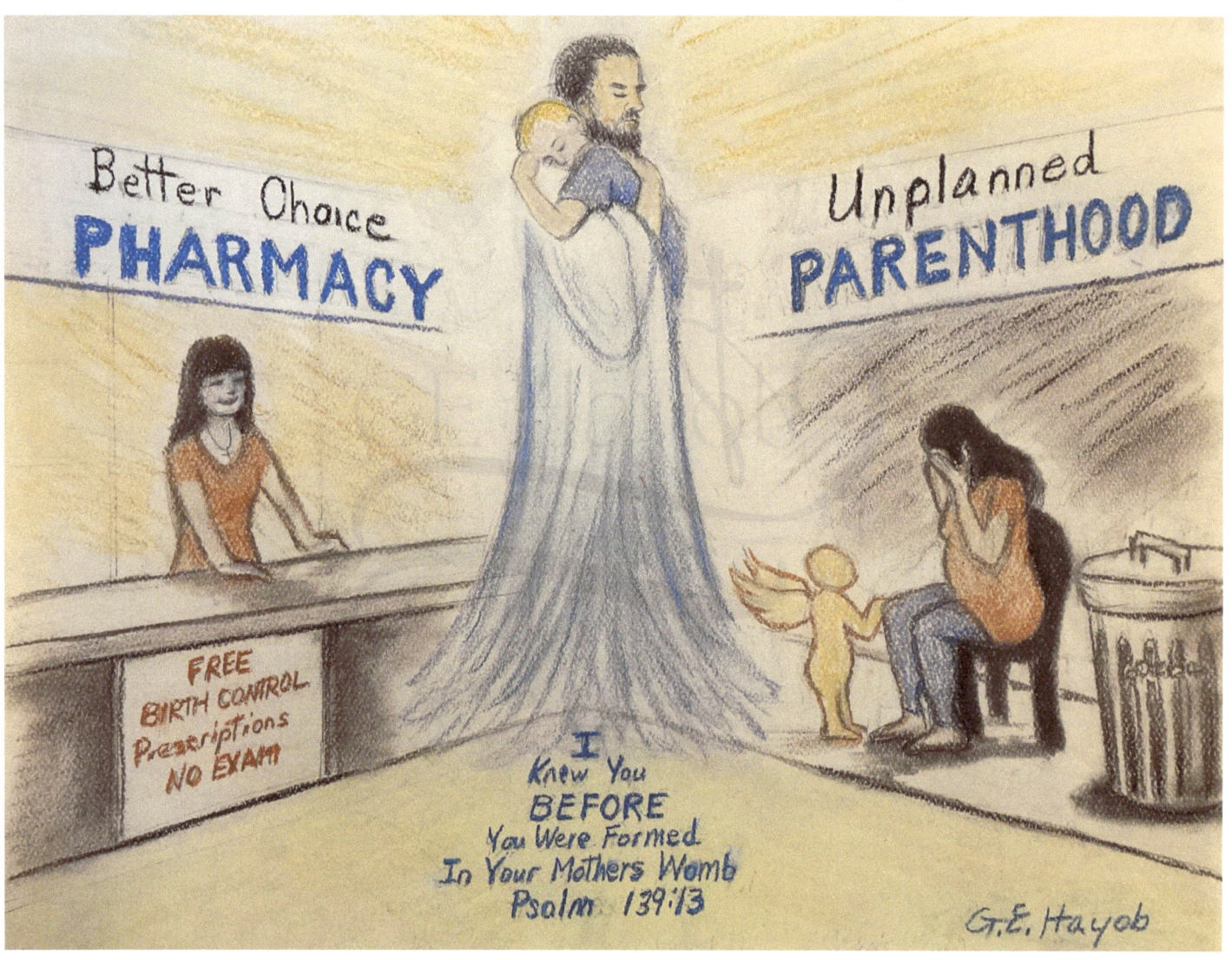

God has a plan for each of our lives. We were never unplanned. You don't have to choose the path that leads to death. You can choose the path that leads to life.

Proverbs 15:24   Psalms 139:15   Acts 10:43

Road Trip

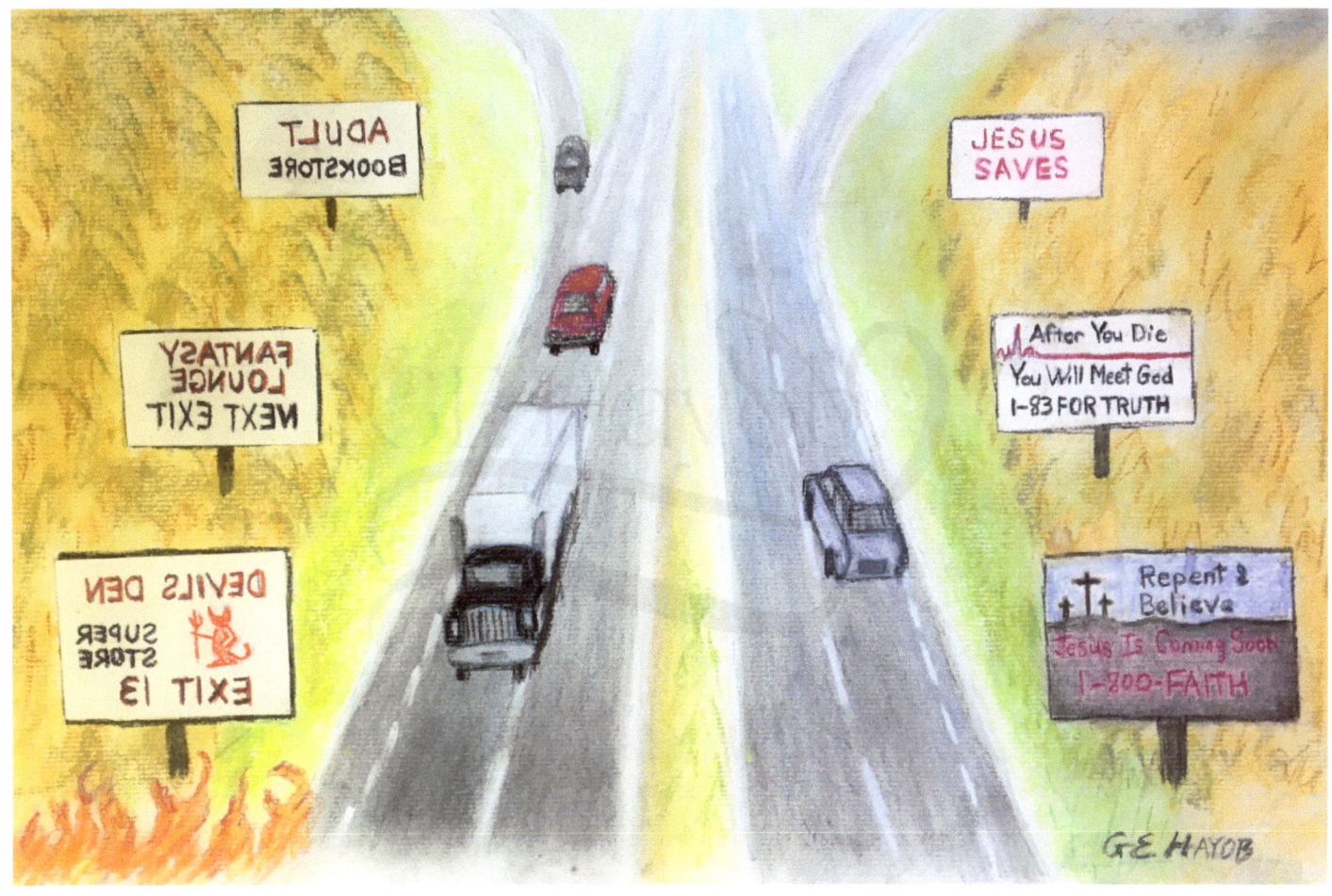

Life is like a long road trip. We are driving in different directions, making our choices. Are the signs and mile markers along your journey taking you on a highway towards a relationship with God or towards a life of sin?

Proverbs 16:17   Matthew 7:13

Come to Me

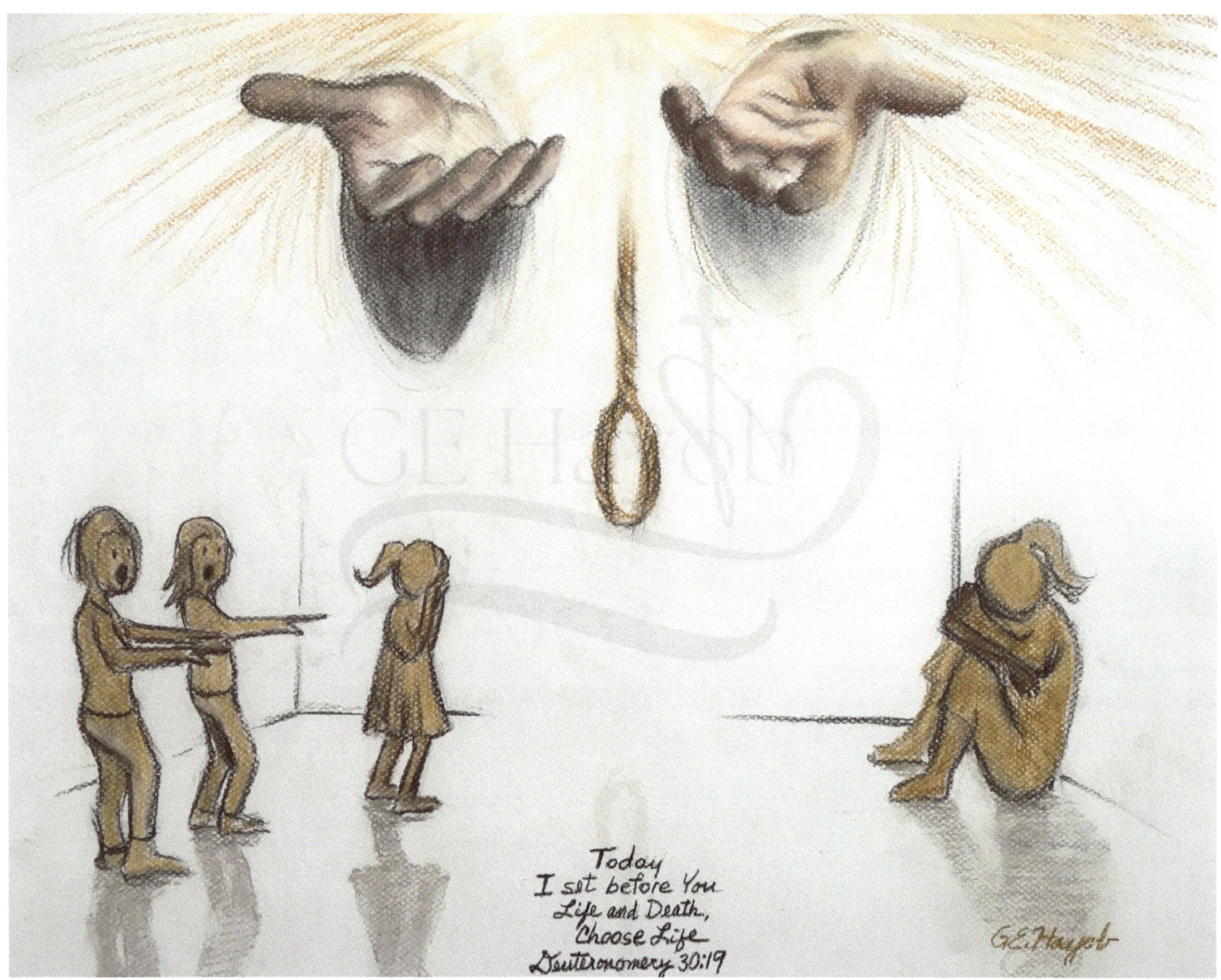

Your life is worth living. Constantly feeling bullied and ridiculed naturally leads to depression and even suicidal thoughts. God created you for more. Choose life and discover the abundant life He has for you.

Proverbs 21:21   Deuteronomy 31:6

Come to Me - 2020

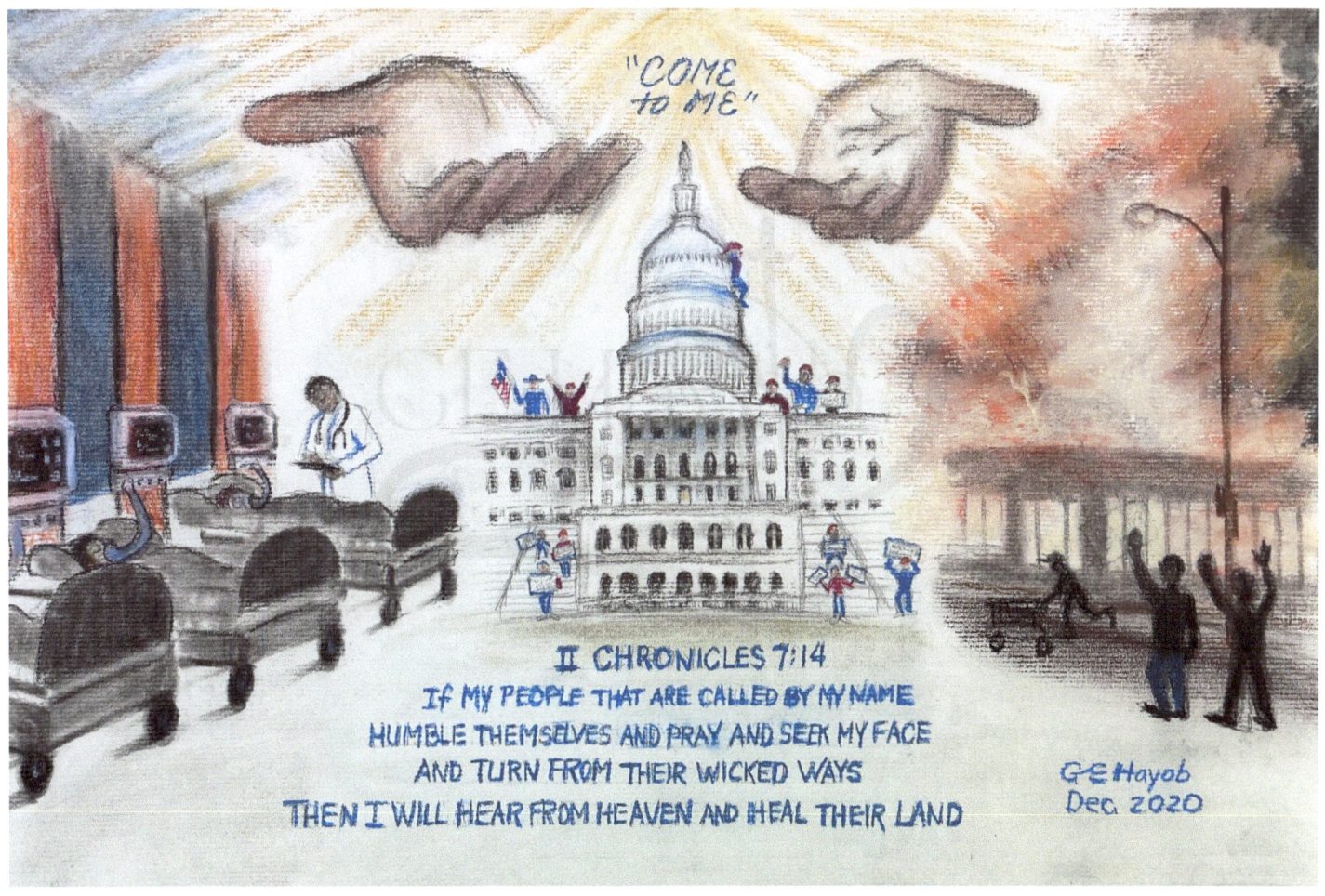

This world is full of pain and grief. The only way to find true peace and rest is in God. He sent his Son, Jesus, to take the punishment for our sins so we could live a full life with God, now and for eternity.

Matthew 11:28   John 3:16

Where Will You Spend Eternity?

I wanted to be a blessing to you, so I am writing this letter because I care about your eternal destiny. Please know that God loves you and he has a great plan for your life. I have a very important question. If today were your last day on earth, do you know for sure, beyond a shadow of a doubt, that you would go to Heaven? The good news is that there is a way to know for sure and it is not through our good deeds.

The Bible reads, "For all have sinned and come short of the glory of God"(Romans 3:23). Which means we all sin and make choices for our lives that go against God's commandments. Because of that sin, we do not deserve to live with God for eternity.

"For the wages of sin is death but the gift of God is eternal life through Jesus Christ our Lord"(Romans 6:23). In reality, we deserve to die the way Jesus died because of our sin. But because of the free gift of Jesus dying in our place and then coming back to life, we can receive a full and abundant life now and forever.

"For whoever calls upon the name of the Lord shall be saved"(Romans 10:13). Whoever means ALL of us. No matter what you have done, the worst decisions and crimes, when you call on the name of Jesus and ask for his forgiveness, you will be saved from spiritual punishment and given the gift of eternal life.

This is my prayer for you:

Lord, I proclaim blessings over the person reading this letter. Do a quick work in their hearts, Jesus, and make yourself known to them. Jesus, comfort them and their loved ones. Fill them with Your peace that passes all understanding. If they never personally called upon the name of the Lord Jesus or if in the past they have, but have turned from you, I pray that they will call upon your name and surrender all to you right now.

Amen.

If you would like to receive the gift God has for you by asking Jesus Christ to come into your life, say this prayer out loud:

Dear Lord Jesus,
you had a choice to go to the cross for me, and now I have a choice to accept your free gift of salvation. Come into my heart and my life. Forgive me of my sins. Wash me and cleanse me of the sin that made my life so dirty. Set me free and change me. Make me the person that You called me to be. Jesus, thank you that you died for me and shed your blood for me. I believe that God raised you from the dead and I thank you that you're coming back again for me. Fill me with boldness to preach the Gospel of Jesus Christ. I am saved. I am born-again. I am forgiven and I am on my way to Heaven because I have Jesus.

Thank you, Jesus.

Amen.

When you asked Jesus to come into your life and to forgive you, He heard you and did so. All of your sins are now forgiven. Always remember to run to God and not from Him because He loves you and has a great plan for your life. That's VERY Good News!

Next steps:

Pray first and ask the Holy Spirit to enlighten you.

Get a Bible. Many churches have Bibles for free or you can download a Bible app or go online. Start reading in the Gospel of John. You can underline Jesus' words in red and highlight any verses or words that speak to you. If there is something you don't understand, ask the Holy Spirit to help you and/or speak to a trusted pastor or friend. Read thru to Revelation and then do it again, this time as a study.

Study His Word DAILY.

> "Man does not live by bread alone but by every word that proceeds from the mouth of God."
> Matthew 4:4

Exhibit for loan, book signing or speaking engagements: Contact artist
All artwork is copyrighted.
Individual prints can be ordered upon request.
Revision - December 2025

Donations going to various Christian Organizations and Charities

Transformation

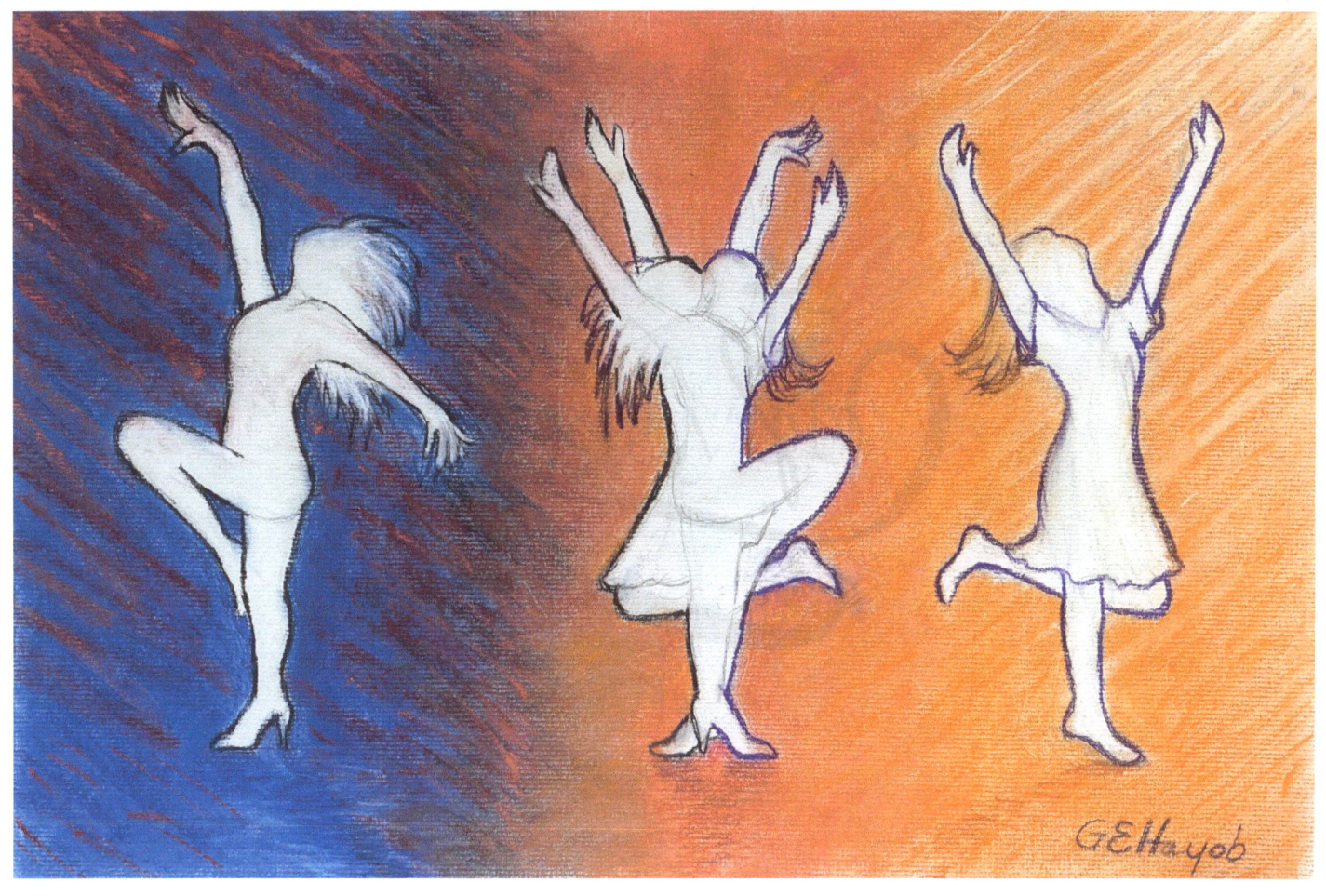

Allow God to transform your life, so you can take off the sin of your present choices and be changed into the person God created you to be, whole and new.

Proverbs 10:24-25   Ephesians 4:22-24

www.ingramcontent.com/pod-product-compliance
Lightning Source LLC
Chambersburg PA
CBHW051825210526
45473CB00005B/1739